The Best For You

Written and Illustrated by
Kelsey Stewart

AuthorHouse™
1663 Liberty Drive
Bloomington, IN 47403
www.authorhouse.com
Phone: 1-800-839-8640

First published by AuthorHouse 10/2/2009

ISBN: 978-1-4490-0832-1 (sc)

Printed in the United States of America
Bloomington, Indiana

authorHOUSE®

This is a story about love. This is a story
about a gift from God that became an even
greater gift to a family. This is a story about
a beautiful baby whom I gave birth to.
This is a story about you.

When I was a young girl, I dreamed of being a mom with my own children. Like every girl, I was married to Prince Charming, who was the perfect husband. I used to spend time playing mommy in my mini kitchen, taking care of my babies in their high chairs. I wanted a house, a good marriage, and a family; that was my dream.

I was not married when I became pregnant with you. I was young and just beginning my adult life. I knew that I wanted you to have both a mother and a father. I knew that I wanted you to have a secure family life. I knew that I wanted you to be happy.

Sometimes in life we are faced with choices. Some of these choices are small: Do you choose the green apple or the red apple? Do you go to the park or to a movie? Other choices are big: Should you play baseball or soccer? Should you stand up for your friend, or should you be afraid of the bully like everyone else?

I was faced with a very difficult choice. I could keep you and raise you myself, or I could search for the right parents that would raise you with their family. There were so many things that I had to think about. I was not just thinking about myself, I was also thinking about you. Most importantly, I was thinking about what would be best for you.

I thought about how wonderful it would be to welcome you into this world. I imagined the wonder of your first laugh. I thought of how great it would be to see your first steps. I imagined how amazing it would be to just be with you, hold you, and love you.

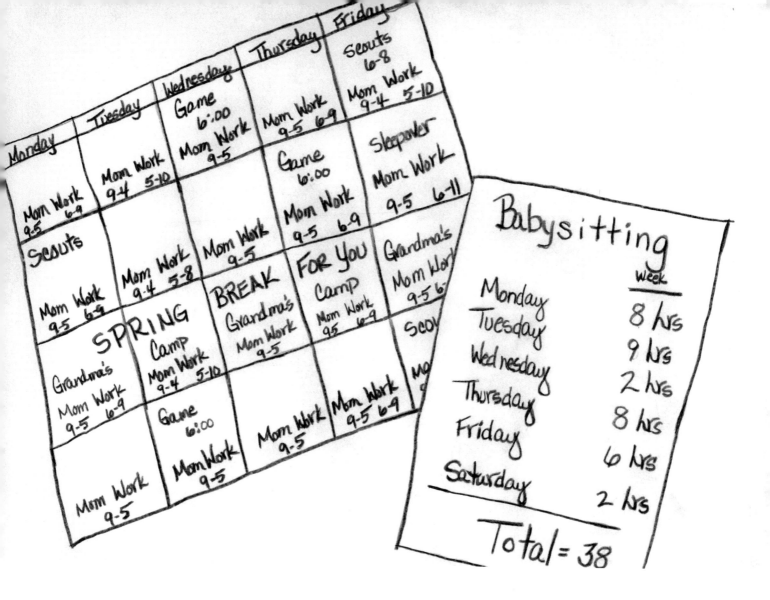

Calendar

Monday	Tuesday	Wednesday	Thursday	Friday
		Game 6:00 / Mom Work 9-5	Mom Work 9-5 6-9	Scouts 6-8 / Mom Work 9-4 5-10
Mom Work 9-5 6-9	Mom Work 9-4 5-10		Game 6:00 / Mom Work 9-5 6-9	Sleepover / Mom Work 9-5 6-11
Scouts / Mom Work 9-5 6-9	Mom Work 9-4 5-8	Mom Work 9-5	BREAK Grandma's / Mom Work 9-5	FOR YOU Camp / Mom Work 9-5 6-9	Grandma's Mom Work 9-5 6-
Grandma's Mom Work 9-5 6-9	SPRING Camp / Mom Work 9-4 5-10				Scou
Mom Work 9-5	Game 6:00 / Mom Work 9-5	Mom Work 9-5	Mom Work 9-5 6-9	Mo

Babysitting

	week
Monday	8 hrs
Tuesday	9 hrs
Wednesday	2 hrs
Thursday	8 hrs
Friday	6 hrs
Saturday	2 hrs
Total	**38**

I thought about our future. I had not finished college. Without a degree I would probably have to work long hours or more than one job to provide for us. All that extra work would mean less time with you. I would want to spend as much time with you as possible.

I then thought of the most important thing about having you. I was not married, and that meant that you would be raised without a dad. I think all children deserve both a mom and a dad to guide them through life. This was the one thing I could not provide, and I decided to find a mom and a dad for you.

So I began to search for the best family that
I could find. I wanted your parents to be in
love and in a good marriage, and I wanted them
to have their own home. I wanted your family
to be happy and fun to be around. I wanted
your family to love you as much as I did.

I found the perfect parents, and they were very excited about you! They were just what I had wanted for you. They told all of their friends and family that they were going to be bringing a baby home. Everyone was so happy to be welcoming you into the world.

I took very good care of myself. As you grew, I loved
feeling you kick around in my belly.., and sometimes
it tickled. I loved to rub my belly and hug you. I
loved hearing your heartbeat at the doctor's office.
I fell in love with you before you were born.

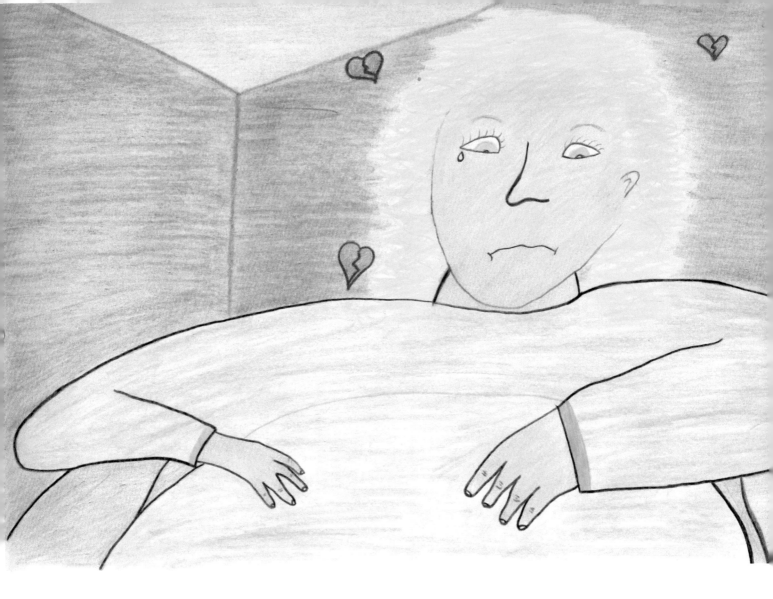

Knowing that I would give birth to you but not raise you was making me very sad. I began to wonder if maybe you would think that I did not love you. There was nothing that was further from the truth. I loved you very much indeed!

So every night before I went to bed I would rub my belly and say, "Hello, I am your mother. I love you very much, with all of my heart. But I cannot take care of you the way that you deserve. I want you to be happy in life, and I am going to do something very brave.

"I am placing you with a wonderful family. They will love you and take care of you for me. You will always be in my heart no matter where I am or what I do. I have made this decision because I want the best for you."

14

Your birthday was a great day. Not only were
you born, but a whole new family was born as
well. Your parents were awfully proud of you.
They were there as soon as you were born. I
thought you were amazing … tiny … beautiful.

When it came time for you to leave the hospital, I was brave like I had said I would be. I hugged you, and then I handed you to your mom. I asked your parents to take care of you and love you every day. I also asked that they always tell you just how much I love you.

You went home with your family, and I went home to mine. I think about you all the time, and I am not sad about my decision, because you are happy. I hope you enjoyed the story of you. I tell your story all the time because it is a wonderful story. I am proud of you, and it shows.

Always know that I love you. Adoption does not mean that I gave up. Adoption does not mean you were not loved or not wanted. Adoption means you have more than one family who loves you. Adoption means you will always be in my heart, whatever I may do. Adoption means I wanted the best for you.

About the Author

Kelsey Stewart is a first-time author/illustrator who has a unique perspective on adoption. She has been through two adoptions as a birth mother and hopes that this book will help children and adults everywhere understand why a mother might choose to place her child for adoption. Kelsey has lived a full, productive, and happy life since her journey as a mother began and considers herself incredibly blessed. She currently resides in Southern California with her husband and their two sons.

Made in the USA
Middletown, DE
21 May 2018